GOLF
LOGBOOK

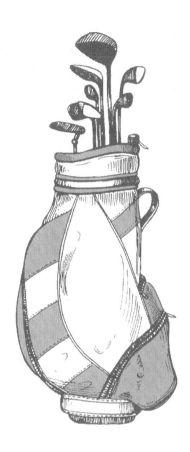

If found, please contact

Name: _____

Tel: _____

Email: _____

Table of Content

Important Dates

Notes

MY TARGETS

Current Handicap

Target Handicap

Current Date:

Current Averages

Fairways Hit	
GIRs	
Up & Downs	
3-Putts	
No./Putts	
Penalties	
Average Score	

Date Achieved:

Target Averages

Fairways Hit	
GIRs	
Up & Downs	
3-Putts	
No./Putts	
Penalties	
Target Score	

AREA FOR IMPROVEMENT

NOTES ON PROGRESS

MY TARGETS

Current Handicap

Target Handicap

Current Date:

Current Averages

Fairways Hit	
GIRs	
Up & Downs	
3-Putts	
No./Putts	
Penalties	
Average Score	

Date Achieved:

Target Averages

Fairways Hit	
GIRs	
Up & Downs	
3-Putts	
No./Putts	
Penalties	
Target Score	

AREA FOR IMPROVEMENT

MY TARGETS

Current Handicap

Target Handicap

Current Date:	Date Achieved:
Current Averages	**Target Averages**

Current Averages		Target Averages	
Fairways Hit		Fairways Hit	
GIRs		GIRs	
Up & Downs		Up & Downs	
3-Putts		3-Putts	
No./Putts		No./Putts	
Penalties		Penalties	
Average Score		Target Score	

AREA FOR IMPROVEMENT

NOTES ON PROGRESS

MY TARGETS

Current Handicap

Target Handicap

Current Date :		Date Achieved:	
Current Averages		**Target Averages**	
Fairways Hit		Fairways Hit	
GIRs		GIRs	
Up & Downs		Up & Downs	
3-Putts		3-Putts	
No./Putts		No./Putts	
Penalties		Penalties	
Average Score		Target Score	

AREA FOR IMPROVEMENT

NOTES ON PROGRESS

MY YARDAGES

Date:

CLUB	HEAD WIND	TAIL WIND	NO WIND
Driver			
3-Wood			
3-Hybrid			
4-Hybrid			
5-Iron			
6-Iron			
7-Iron			
8-Iron			
9-Iron			
PW			
GW			
SW			
LW			

MY YARDAGES

Date:

CLUB	HEAD WIND	TAIL WIND	NO WIND
Driver			
3-Wood			
3-Hybrid			
4-Hybrid			
5-Iron			
6-Iron			
7-Iron			
8-Iron			
9-Iron			
PW			
GW			
SW			
LW			

MY YARDAGES

Date:

CLUB	HEAD WIND	TAIL WIND	NO WIND
Driver			
3-Wood			
3-Hybrid			
4-Hybrid			
5-Iron			
6-Iron			
7-Iron			
8-Iron			
9-Iron			
PW			
GW			
SW			
LW			

MY YARDAGES

Date:

CLUB	HEAD WIND	TAIL WIND	NO WIND
Driver			
3-Wood			
3-Hybrid			
4-Hybrid			
5-Iron			
6-Iron			
7-Iron			
8-Iron			
9-Iron			
PW			
GW			
SW			
LW			

GAME SCORES

Course:

Date: Tee Off Time:

Handicap:

Par:

Yardage:

Slope:

Rating:

Weather

Conditions:

Temperature:

Wind:

Casual

Competition

9 Holes

18 Holes

Players

Front 9

	1	2	3	4	5	6	7	8	9	TOTAL
PAR										
SCORE										
TEE BOX										
YARDAGE										
FW										
GIRs										
U&D										
PUTTS										
PENALTIES										

Back 9

	1	2	3	4	5	6	7	8	9	TOTAL	GRAND TOTAL
PAR											
SCORE											
TEE BOX											
YARDAGE											
FW											
GIRs											
U&D											
PUTTS											
PENALTIES											

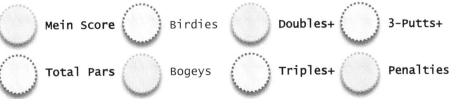

Mein Score   Birdies   Doubles+   3-Putts+

Total Pars   Bogeys   Triples+   Penalties

Notes about this Course

Notes about my Performance

Notes from the 19th Hole

GAME SCORES

Course:

Date: Tee Off Time:

Weather

Handicap:

Par:

Yardage:

Slope:

Rating:

Conditions:

Temperature:

Wind:

Casual

Competition

9 Holes

18 Holes

Players

Front 9

	1	2	3	4	5	6	7	8	9	TOTAL
PAR										
SCORE										
TEE BOX										
YARDAGE										
FW										
GIRs										
U&D										
PUTTS										
PENALTIES										

Back 9

	1	2	3	4	5	6	7	8	9	TOTAL	GRAND TOTAL
PAR											
SCORE											
TEE BOX											
YARDAGE											
FW											
GIRs											
U&D											
PUTTS											
PENALTIES											

Mein Score   Birdies   Doubles+   3-Putts+

Total Pars   Bogeys   Triples+   Penalties

Notes about this Course

Notes about my Performance

Notes from the 19th Hole

GAME SCORES

Course:

Date: Tee Off Time:

Handicap: _____

Par: _____

Yardage: _____

Slope: _____

Rating: _____

Weather

Conditions: _____

Temperature: _____

Wind: _____

◯ Casual

◯ Competition

◯ 9 Holes

◯ 18 Holes

Players

_____

_____

_____

_____

Front 9

	1	2	3	4	5	6	7	8	9	TOTAL
PAR										
SCORE										
TEE BOX										
YARDAGE										
FW										
GIRs										
U&D										
PUTTS										
PENALTIES										

Back 9

	1	2	3	4	5	6	7	8	9	TOTAL	GRAND TOTAL
PAR											
SCORE											
TEE BOX											
YARDAGE											
FW											
GIRs											
U&D											
PUTTS											
PENALTIES											

Mein Score   Birdies   Doubles+   3-Putts+

Total Pars   Bogeys   Triples+   Penalties

Notes about this Course

Notes about my Performance

Notes from the 19th Hole

GAME SCORES

Course:

Date: Tee Off Time:

Weather

Handicap: _____

Par: _____

Yardage: _____

Slope: _____

Rating: _____

Conditions: _____

Temperature: _____

Wind: _____

○ Casual

○ Competition

○ 9 Holes

○ 18 Holes

Players

_____

_____

_____

_____

Front 9

	1	2	3	4	5	6	7	8	9	TOTAL
PAR										
SCORE										
TEE BOX										
YARDAGE										
FW										
GIRs										
U&D										
PUTTS										
PENALTIES										

Back 9

	1	2	3	4	5	6	7	8	9	TOTAL	GRAND TOTAL
PAR											
SCORE											
TEE BOX											
YARDAGE											
FW											
GIRs											
U&D											
PUTTS											
PENALTIES											

Mein Score   Birdies   Doubles+   3-Putts+

Total Pars   Bogeys   Triples+   Penalties

35

Notes about this Course

Notes about my Performance

Notes from the 19th Hole

GAME SCORES

Course: _____

Date: _____ Tee Off Time: _____

Weather

Conditions: _____

Temperature: _____

Wind: _____

Handicap: _____

Par: _____

Yardage: _____

Slope: _____

Rating: _____

○ Casual

○ Competition

○ 9 Holes

○ 18 Holes

Players

_____

_____

_____

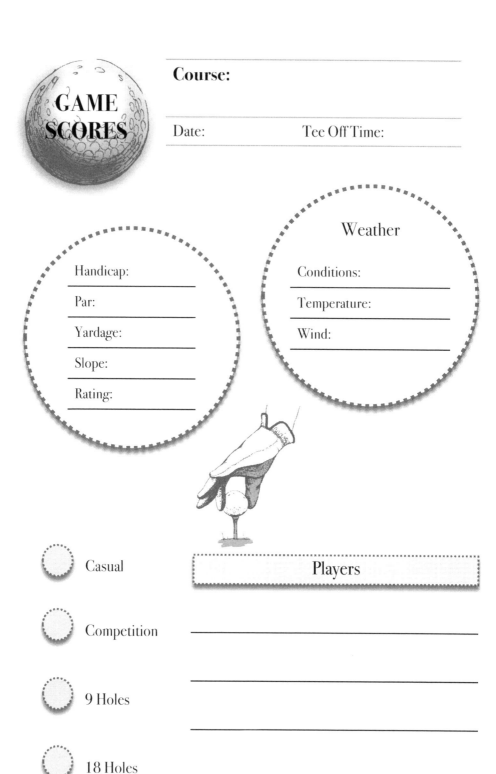

Front 9

	1	2	3	4	5	6	7	8	9	TOTAL
PAR										
SCORE										
TEE BOX										
YARDAGE										
FW										
GIRs										
U&D										
PUTTS										
PENALTIES										

Back 9

	1	2	3	4	5	6	7	8	9	TOTAL	GRAND TOTAL
PAR											
SCORE											
TEE BOX											
YARDAGE											
FW											
GIRs											
U&D											
PUTTS											
PENALTIES											

Mein Score   Birdies   Doubles+   3-Putts+

Total Pars   Bogeys   Triples+   Penalties

Notes about this Course

Notes about my Performance

Notes from the 19th Hole

GAME SCORES

Course:

Date: Tee Off Time:

Handicap:

Par:

Yardage:

Slope:

Rating:

Weather

Conditions:

Temperature:

Wind:

○ Casual

○ Competition

○ 9 Holes

○ 18 Holes

Players

_____

_____

_____

_____

Front 9

	1	2	3	4	5	6	7	8	9	TOTAL
PAR										
SCORE										
TEE BOX										
YARDAGE										
FW										
GIRs										
U&D										
PUTTS										
PENALTIES										

Back 9

	1	2	3	4	5	6	7	8	9	TOTAL	GRAND TOTAL
PAR											
SCORE											
TEE BOX											
YARDAGE											
FW											
GIRs											
U&D											
PUTTS											
PENALTIES											

Mein Score   Birdies   Doubles+   3-Putts+

Total Pars   Bogeys   Triples+   Penalties

Notes about this Course

Notes about my Performance

Notes from the 19th Hole

GAME SCORES

Course:

Date: Tee Off Time:

Weather

Handicap: _____

Par: _____

Yardage: _____

Slope: _____

Rating: _____

Conditions: _____

Temperature: _____

Wind: _____

○ Casual

○ Competition

○ 9 Holes

○ 18 Holes

Players

_____

_____

_____

_____

Front 9

	1	2	3	4	5	6	7	8	9	TOTAL
PAR										
SCORE										
TEE BOX										
YARDAGE										
FW										
GIRs										
U&D										
PUTTS										
PENALTIES										

Back 9

	1	2	3	4	5	6	7	8	9	TOTAL	GRAND TOTAL
PAR											
SCORE											
TEE BOX											
YARDAGE											
FW											
GIRs											
U&D											
PUTTS											
PENALTIES											

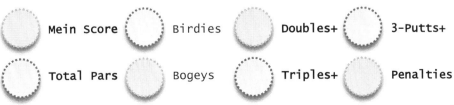

Mein Score   Birdies   Doubles+   3-Putts+

Total Pars   Bogeys   Triples+   Penalties

Notes about this Course

Notes about my Performance

Notes from the 19th Hole

GAME SCORES

Course:

Date: Tee Off Time:

Handicap:

Par:

Yardage:

Slope:

Rating:

Weather

Conditions:

Temperature:

Wind:

○ Casual

○ Competition

○ 9 Holes

○ 18 Holes

Players

_____

_____

_____

_____

Front 9

	1	2	3	4	5	6	7	8	9	TOTAL
PAR										
SCORE										
TEE BOX										
YARDAGE										
FW										
GIRs										
U&D										
PUTTS										
PENALTIES										

Back 9

	1	2	3	4	5	6	7	8	9	TOTAL	GRAND TOTAL
PAR											
SCORE											
TEE BOX											
YARDAGE											
FW											
GIRs											
U&D											
PUTTS											
PENALTIES											

Mein Score   Birdies   Doubles+   3-Putts+

Total Pars   Bogeys   Triples+   Penalties

Notes about this Course

Notes about my Performance

Notes from the 19th Hole

GAME SCORES

Course:

Date: Tee Off Time:

Handicap: _____

Par: _____

Yardage: _____

Slope: _____

Rating: _____

Weather

Conditions: _____

Temperature: _____

Wind: _____

○ Casual

○ Competition

○ 9 Holes

○ 18 Holes

Players

_____

_____

_____

_____

Front 9

	1	2	3	4	5	6	7	8	9	TOTAL
PAR										
SCORE										
TEE BOX										
YARDAGE										
FW										
GIRs										
U&D										
PUTTS										
PENALTIES										

Back 9

	1	2	3	4	5	6	7	8	9	TOTAL	GRAND TOTAL
PAR											
SCORE											
TEE BOX											
YARDAGE											
FW											
GIRs											
U&D											
PUTTS											
PENALTIES											

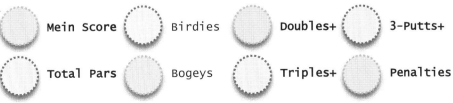

Mein Score   Birdies   Doubles+   3-Putts+

Total Pars   Bogeys   Triples+   Penalties

Notes about this Course

Notes about my Performance

Notes from the 19th Hole

Course:

Date: Tee Off Time:

Handicap: _____

Par: _____

Yardage: _____

Slope: _____

Rating: _____

Weather

Conditions: _____

Temperature: _____

Wind: _____

 Casual

Competition

9 Holes

18 Holes

Players

_____

_____

_____

_____

Front 9

	1	2	3	4	5	6	7	8	9	TOTAL
PAR										
SCORE										
TEE BOX										
YARDAGE										
FW										
GIRs										
U&D										
PUTTS										
PENALTIES										

Back 9

	1	2	3	4	5	6	7	8	9	TOTAL	GRAND TOTAL
PAR											
SCORE											
TEE BOX											
YARDAGE											
FW											
GIRs											
U&D											
PUTTS											
PENALTIES											

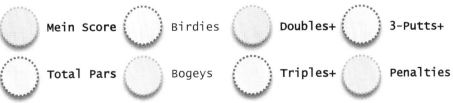

Mein Score Birdies Doubles+ 3-Putts+

Total Pars Bogeys Triples+ Penalties

Notes about this Course

Notes about my Performance

Notes from the 19ᵗʰ Hole

GAME SCORES

Course:

Date: _____ Tee Off Time: _____

Handicap: _____

Par: _____

Yardage: _____

Slope: _____

Rating: _____

Weather

Conditions: _____

Temperature: _____

Wind: _____

○ Casual

○ Competition

○ 9 Holes

○ 18 Holes

Players

_____

_____

_____

_____

Front 9

	1	2	3	4	5	6	7	8	9	TOTAL
PAR										
SCORE										
TEE BOX										
YARDAGE										
FW										
GIRs										
U&D										
PUTTS										
PENALTIES										

Back 9

	1	2	3	4	5	6	7	8	9	TOTAL	GRAND TOTAL
PAR											
SCORE											
TEE BOX											
YARDAGE											
FW											
GIRs											
U&D											
PUTTS											
PENALTIES											

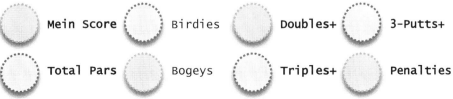

Mein Score   Birdies   Doubles+   3-Putts+

Total Pars   Bogeys   Triples+   Penalties

Notes about this Course

Notes about my Performance

Notes from the 19th Hole

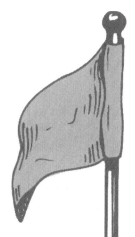

Tournaments

TOURNAMENT TRACKER

Date	Tournament	Course	Entry Fee	Entry Closing Date	Entered ✓

TOURNAMENT TRACKER

Date	Tournament	Course	Entry Fee	Entry Closing Date	Entered ✓

EVENT STATS

Event:

Course:

Date: Tee Off Time:

Entry Fee: Prize:

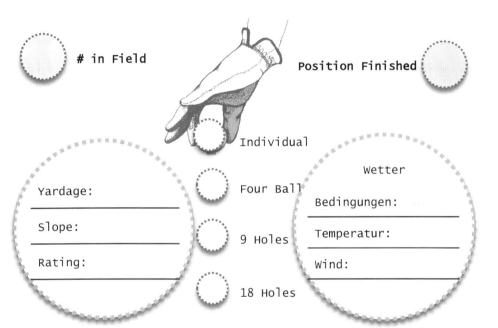

in Field

Position Finished

Individual

Four Ball

9 Holes

18 Holes

Yardage:

Slope:

Rating:

Wetter

Bedingungen:

Temperatur:

Wind:

Players

_____

_____

_____

_____

Scores und Leaderboard

Round	1	2	3	4
Score				
Finished				
TOTAL SCORE				

EVENT STATS

Event:

Course:

Date: Tee Off Time:

Entry Fee: Prize:

in Field

Position Finished

Individual

Four Ball

9 Holes

18 Holes

Yardage:

Slope:

Rating:

Wetter

Bedingungen:

Temperatur:

Wind:

Players

_____

_____

_____

_____

Scores und Leaderboard

Round	1	2	3	4
Score				
Finished				
TOTAL SCORE				

EVENT STATS

Event:

Course:	
Date:	Tee Off Time:
Entry Fee:	Prize:

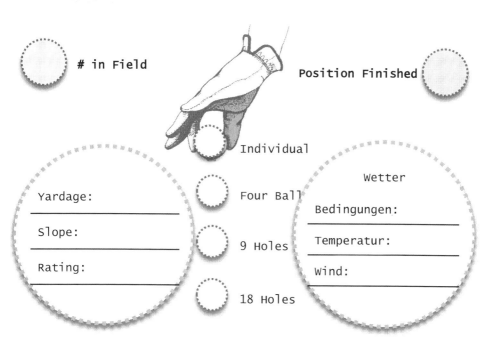

in Field

Position Finished

Individual

Four Ball

9 Holes

18 Holes

Yardage: _____

Slope: _____

Rating: _____

Wetter

Bedingungen: _____

Temperatur: _____

Wind: _____

Players

_____

_____

_____

_____

Scores und Leaderboard

Round	1	2	3	4
Score				
Finished				
TOTAL SCORE				

EVENT STATS

Event:

Course:

Date: Tee Off Time:

Entry Fee: Prize:

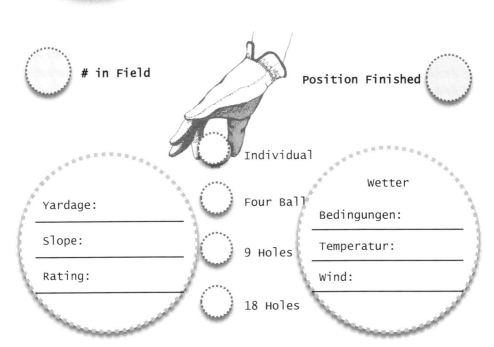

in Field

Position Finished

Individual

Yardage:

Slope:

Rating:

Four Ball

9 Holes

18 Holes

Wetter

Bedingungen:

Temperatur:

Wind:

Players

_____

_____

_____

_____

Scores und Leaderboard

Round	1	2	3	4
Score				
Finished				
TOTAL SCORE				

EVENT STATS

Event:

Course:

Date: Tee Off Time:

Entry Fee: Prize:

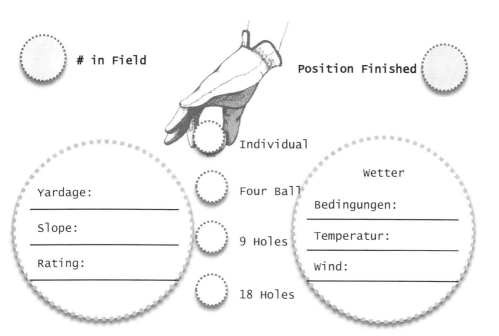

 # in Field

Position Finished

Individual

Yardage: _____

Slope: _____

Rating: _____

Four Ball

9 Holes

18 Holes

Wetter

Bedingungen: _____

Temperatur: _____

Wind: _____

Players

_____

_____

_____

_____

Scores und Leaderboard

Round	1	2	3	4
Score				
Finished				
TOTAL SCORE				

FINANCE

Date	Details (Equipment, Tournament, 19th Hole)	Budget		Actual	

Date	Details	Budget		Actual	

FINANCE

Date	Details	Budget		Actual